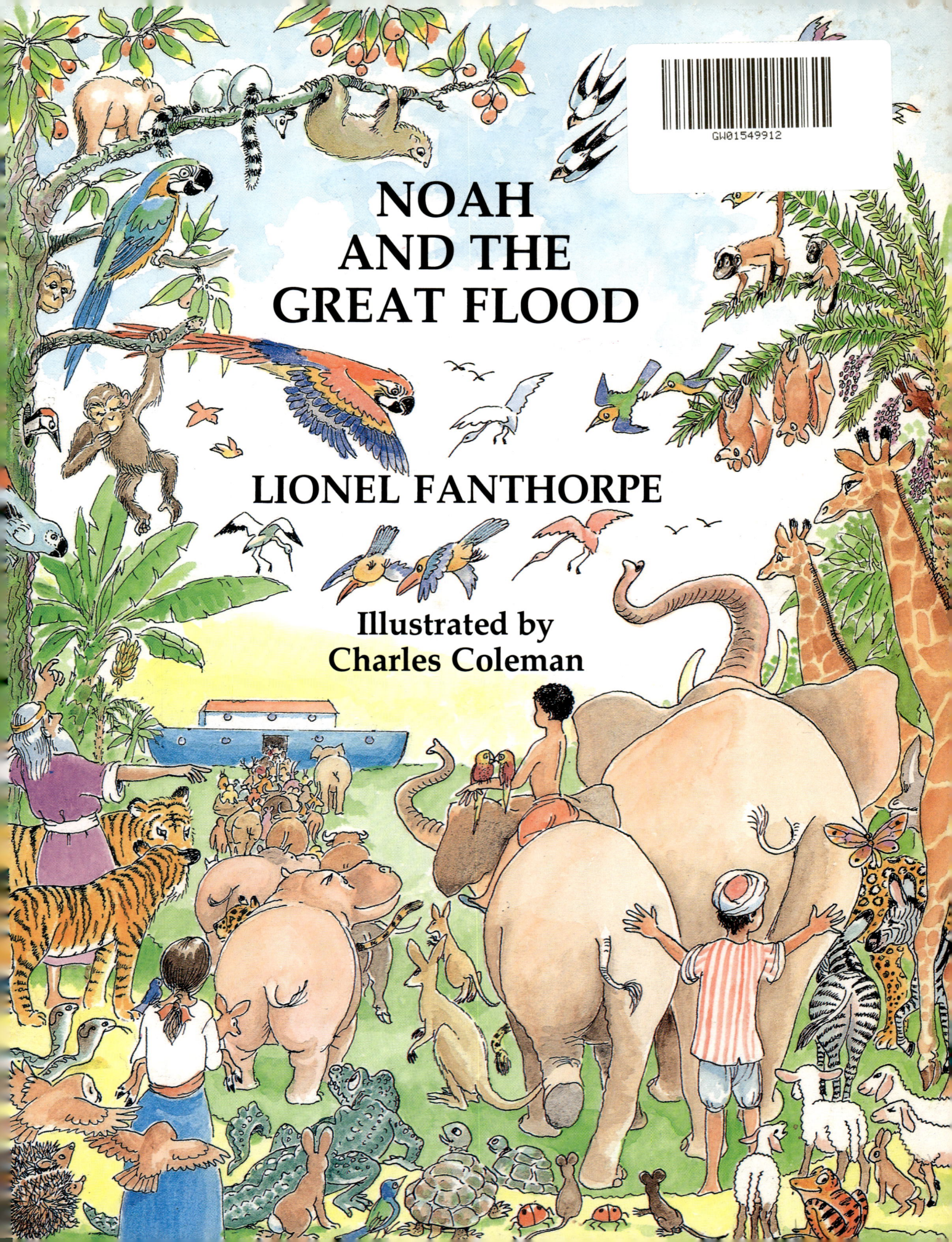

This book is dedicated to our friends John and Barbara Kirby of Norfolk: good, kind and caring people who have as much concern about animals as Noah had.

ISBN 1 85219 062 0

© (1992) Lionel Fanthorpe

British Library Cataloguing in Publication Data
A catalogue record for this book is
available from the British Library

All rights reserved. No part of this publication may be reproduced, stored in a retrieval system or transmitted, in any form or by any means, electronic, mechanical, photocopying, recording or otherwise, without prior permission of the copyright owner.

All enquires and requests relevent to this title should be sent to the publisher, Bishopsgate Press Ltd, Bartholomew House, 15 Tonbridge Road, Hildenborough, Kent TN11 9BH

Printed in Singapore through GlobalCom Pte Ltd

CONTENTS

Foreword by Canon Mogford	4
Before the Flood	5
Noah Listens to God	6
Noah Begins to Build the Ark	8
Noah Collects the Animals	10
Noah Loads the Animals	12
The Rain Begins	14
The Ark Floats Away	16
Noah and his Family Care for the Animals	18
The Rain Stops	20
The Ark Lands Safely on Mount Ararat	22
Noah Sends out the Raven	24
Noah Sends out the Dove	26
Noah Sets the Animals Free	28
Noah and his Family leave the Ark	30
The Rainbow Sign	32

FOREWORD

by Canon S.H. Mogford

Bible stories are part of our heritage and have been told and retold all down the centuries. They are recited as facts by some; for others their value will always lie in the moral they illustrate. For the truly discerning they can be both. Whoever attempts it anew is a brave writer indeed. Nothing is more difficult than to make the old and tried new and interesting, and the too familiar still seem exciting to hear or read. The pen of any such writer has to look all the time to the guiding hand of Almighty God.

The Reverend Lionel Fanthorpe has his own individual approach to these old stories, already evident in his earlier volume in the same series, *Joseph: Dreamer, Prisoner and Provider*. There is a gentle skill in his use of words for his young readers, easy to remember rhymes for those with alert memories, and a reverence and dignity of touch both for his subject and his readers.

How lucky he continues to be to have an illustrator as gifted as Charles Coleman. Together they will surely earn for themselves an honoured place in the field of religious writing for small children.

BEFORE THE FLOOD

The Great Flood happened a very long time ago. Before the flood many people were not living good lives: they were selfish and unkind; they stole from one another; they did not tell the truth; they did not help sick people; they did not look after old people; they did not give any money to the poor.

NOAH LISTENS TO GOD

Among all these bad, selfish people, there lived one good man. His name was Noah. He had a wife and three sons named Ham, Shem and Japheth. All the sons were married. The people in Noah's family were good like he was.

One day God told Noah that a great flood would come. He told Noah to build an ark, a very large boat, which would save him and his family when the flood came.

Because Noah was a good man he always did his best to do what God said.

POEM

"Listen, my sons, and listen well:
I have important news to tell.
God has warned me that floods will come,
And they will wash away our home.
So bring your mother; tell your wives.
God has a plan to save our lives:
We have to build an ark, or boat.
And on the waters it shall float.
We must work hard. We must be brave.
Animals too we have to save."
Noah's family all agreed
To help him build the Ark with speed.

PRAYER

Dear Lord,
Help us to hear
Your call,
And to answer
Quickly and willingly
Like Noah did.
Amen.

NOAH BEGINS TO BUILD THE ARK

God gave Noah all the details he needed to build the ark: it was to be 140 metres long, 23 metres wide and nearly 14 metres high.

In Noah's time these measurements were given in cubits: a cubit is the distance from your outstretched fingertips to your elbow.

Noah and his family worked hard with saws and hammers, cutting the wood to shape and fitting it together. It would be nice to think that some of the animals who would be saved by the Ark also helped to build it. Perhaps they did.

POEM

The saw goes "Buzz!"
The hammer goes "Bang!"
The wood goes "Thud!"
The iron goes "Clang!"
With busy hands and busy feet
We soon will make the ark complete.
Working away in wind and sun —
God will protect us till it's done.

PRAYER

Dear Lord Jesus,
When You were with us on earth,
As one of us,
You worked as a Carpenter in Nazareth.
Help us to do our work well,
For You and for others.
Amen.

NOAH COLLECTS THE ANIMALS

God told Noah to save all kinds of animals as well as his family. Noah and his wife, his sons and their wives, gathered the animals together gently and led them into the Ark. They also took large supplies of food on board: enough to last until the Great Flood was over.

POEM

Look to your left: look to your right.
Are many animals in sight?
Don't let them wander, stop or stray.
Shepherd them safely; come this way.

Gently push them and gently pull:
We won't stop till the Ark is full.
Camel and tiger; cat and dog —
Please don't forget my friend the frog!
Although a frog knows how to swim,
I've saved a place up here for him.

PRAYER

Dear Lord,
Help us always to be kind to animals,
As your servant Noah was,
Because the animals
Are Your creatures too.
Amen.

NOAH LOADS THE ANIMALS

Noah and his family made sure that all the animals which God had told them to take with them were safely on board.
After that the animals had to be put into their proper stalls and cages ready for the long voyage when the great flood came.
Noah and his family also had to take all kinds of food on board so that all the different animals would have enough to eat.

POEM

I have got a bed of straw,
Soft and warm across my floor.
And my neighbour's got one too.
I think he's a kangaroo.
Quite nearby I see a snake:
Big bright eyes show he's awake.
Elephants! I can see two
Filling up our floating zoo.
Someone standing close to me
Has a neck just like a tree.
When I look at him I laugh —
I think that he is a giraffe.

PRAYER

Dear Lord and Father of us all,
You made us all different,
But You love us all the same.
Whether we are boys or girls,
Tall or short,
Black, brown or white.
We are all just as dear to You.
Thank You for making us different.
Help us to love one another.
As You love us.
Amen.

THE RAIN BEGINS

As soon as the animals were safely settled, Noah and his family got on board too. God himself closed up the Ark securely, and then the rain began.

Hour after hour, day after day, the rain fell. The oceans, rivers and lakes rose higher and higher until one big sheet of water met another.

The Ark began to float on the ever-rising flood. Noah and his family and all the animals were safe inside.

POEM

Day after day the rain came down.
It covered village, field and town.
Higher and higher rose the flood
Till everything was rain and mud.

Inside the Ark, all safe and dry.
Noah and his family floated high.
The animals kept looking round:
They saw the flood but no dry ground.

PRAYER

Teach us, dear Lord
To trust in You always,
Whatever happens,
Just as Noah
And his family
Trusted in You
When the Great Flood came.
Amen.

THE ARK FLOATS AWAY

Because Noah had done exactly what God told him to do the Ark was perfect for its very important job. It was built in just the right way, so it floated safely on the flood.

Day after day, night after night, Noah and his family and all the animals floated along.

The people were very busy looking after the animals: keeping them clean, well fed, calm and happy, and watching over them while they slept.

POEM

Gently floating on the tide . . .
Softly . . . quietly . . . they ride . . .
Moving with the current's flow . . .
On their peaceful way they go . . .
Snug and warm they fall asleep . . .
Noah his faithful watch will keep.

PRAYER

Dear Lord,
You keep a loving watch over us
As Noah and his family
Kept watch over the animals
In the Ark.
Please take care of us,
And all whom we love,
As we journey over
The wide waters of life.
We ask it for Jesus' sake.
Amen.

NOAH AND HIS FAMILY CARE FOR THE ANIMALS

Animals are very lovely, but they have to be looked after carefully *every day*. Taking care of them can be very hard work, and it can also take a lot of our time.

Noah and his family were *very busy* feeding the animals; cleaning them; grooming them and stroking them to keep them calm and happy on the long voyage.

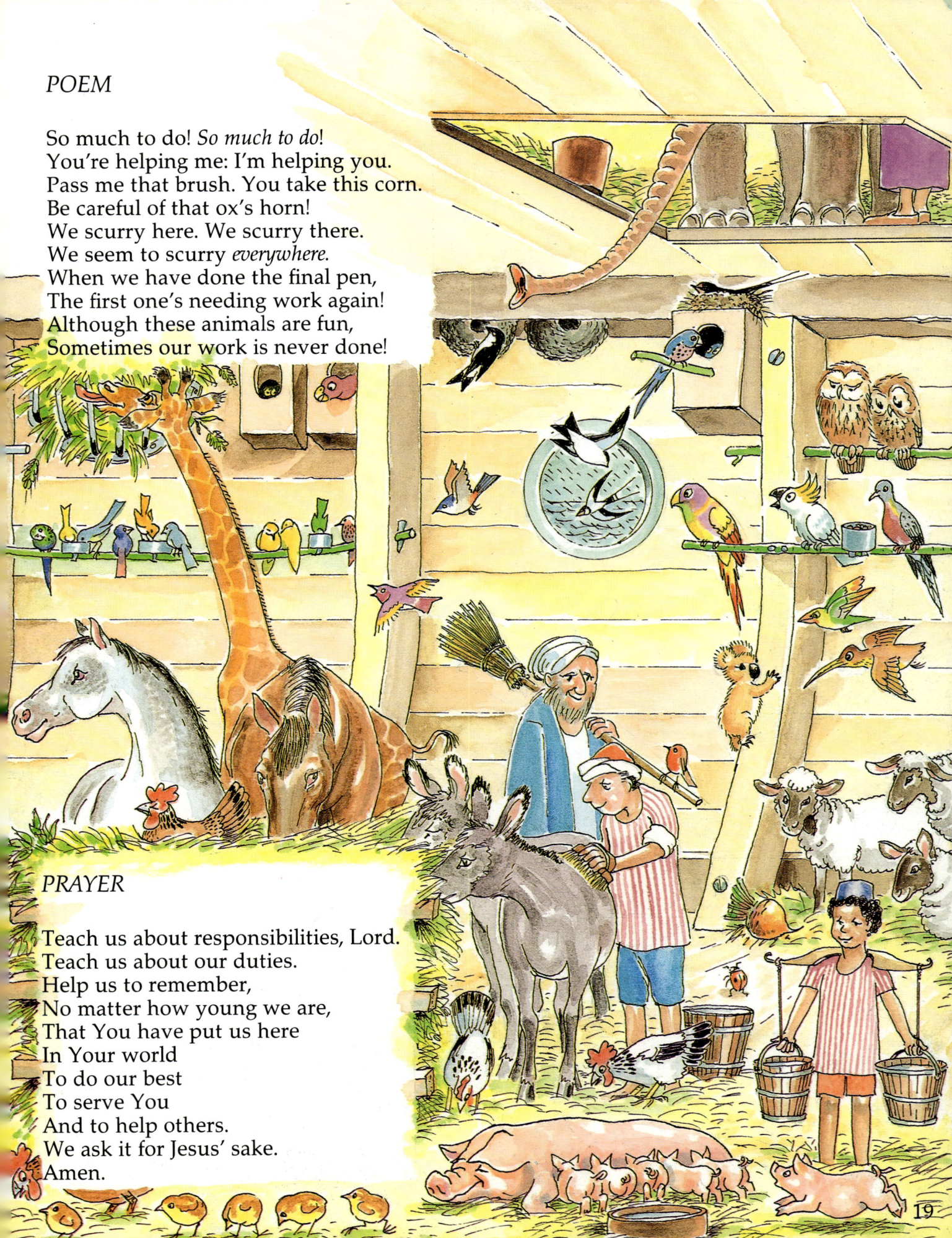

POEM

So much to do! *So much to do!*
You're helping me: I'm helping you.
Pass me that brush. You take this corn.
Be careful of that ox's horn!
We scurry here. We scurry there.
We seem to scurry *everywhere*.
When we have done the final pen,
The first one's needing work again!
Although these animals are fun,
Sometimes our work is never done!

PRAYER

Teach us about responsibilities, Lord.
Teach us about our duties.
Help us to remember,
No matter how young we are,
That You have put us here
In Your world
To do our best
To serve You
And to help others.
We ask it for Jesus' sake.
Amen.

THE RAIN STOPS

The Bible tells us that it rained for forty days and forty nights without stopping at all. Think how wet everything gets after just *one day's* heavy rain. Try to imagine a *whole week's* rain. Then guess how wet it would be if it rained for nearly *six weeks*! Forty days is roughly the length of the long summer holiday from school. Think of how much rain would fall *if it rained every day of the long summer holiday.*

Then, *at last*, the rain stopped. How much quieter it must have seemed in the Ark after that.

POEM

Forty days and nights of rain!
Will it *never* stop?
Every day is just the same:
Listen to it drop!

Every minute, every hour:
Will it *never* stop?
Was there ever such a shower?
Listen to it drop!

Forty days and forty nights:
Will it *never* stop?
Listen! I can't hear it now!
That was the last drop!

PRAYER

Lord of all Strength,
Lord of all Endurance,
Help us to be strong;
Help us to endure;
Help us to put up with difficult things
That go on for a long time,
Like the rain did
When Noah was in the Ark.
Jesus endured terrible things
For our sake.
Help us to endure our small troubles
For His sake.
Amen.

THE ARK LANDS SAFELY ON MOUNT ARARAT

Even after the rain had stopped it took several months for the flood water to go down. Very slowly it got lower and lower until one day Noah, his family, and all the animals felt a gentle bump and heard a soft grating sound. The Ark had touched solid ground again. They had landed safely on Mount Ararat, but there was still nothing to be seen but water all round them.

POEM

It's over! We've landed!
We've done it! We're down!
God's great Ark has saved us —
We're not going to drown!
Sing praises and thanks; first
To God, then to Noah.
We will know where we are
When the water sinks lower.

PRAYER

Loving and caring Father,
You have looked after us
Since the day we were born.
You have guided us
And guarded us,
As you guided and guarded
Your servant Noah.
Please go on taking care of us,
Our families and our friends,
Today, tomorrow and always,
For Jesus' sake.
Amen.

NOAH SENDS OUT THE RAVEN

Noah had a good idea for finding out whether the flood waters had gone down far enough for any dry land to appear. He sent out a big black bird called a raven. The raven made only short flights backwards and forwards in all directions. It kept coming back to the Ark because it could not see anywhere to land.

POEM

The big, black wings were weak and slow:
He was not used to flight.
Darker than storm clouds — up he climbed —
Darker than starless night.
"There goes my raven!" shouted Noah.
"I wonder what he'll find.
I wonder if he will return,
Or leave us all behind."
Forward and back the raven flew,
Westward, then east again.
His bright eyes darted north and south,
But looked for land in vain.

PRAYER

Dear Lord,
You lived on earth with us,
As One of us;
You know how hard it is
To go on looking for things
When someone is tired and longing to rest.
Help us to go on searching for You
And Your Kingdom until we find You,
Because that is *The Most Important Search of All*.
Amen.

NOAH SENDS OUT THE DOVE

Because the raven had had no success, Noah decided to send out a dove.

For a time the dove had no success either, then it came back to Noah with a freshly picked olive leaf in its beak. This told Noah that the dove must have found some dry land somewhere.

POEM

"Away, my gentle friend with wings,
Across this water search for things."
So Noah stretched forth his strong right hand,
But looked in vain for sight of land.
The dove gave Noah a gentle "Coo,"
Which meant, "I'll do my best for you."
It flew till it was out of sight.
Noah prayed that it would be all right.
With olive twig the dove returned:
Something important Noah had learned.
The dove had not gone out in vain:
Somewhere the earth was dry again.

PRAYER

Dear Lord,
Your servant Noah
Was full of hope
When he sent out
That brave and gentle dove.
Fill us with hope,
Like Noah had,
And make us brave and gentle,
Like the dove.
For Jesus' sake,
Amen.

NOAH SETS THE ANIMALS FREE

The waters went down slowly and steadily. More and more dry land appeared. At last there was enough room for Noah to let out all the animals. How they enjoyed their freedom after being shut up in the Ark for so long! Monkeys and squirrels climbed. Lions and tigers bounded as they ran. Kangaroos and frogs hopped and jumped as high as they could. Owls glided in wide circles, blinking as they flew. Bright little kingfishers darted here and there. Ducks, geese and swans swam. Snakes wriggled. Moles dug tunnels. Each was happy in his own way.

POEM

The water's gone and we're free at last.
Excuse me, please, as I hurry past.
All of us eager to use our limbs:
The lion bounds and the penguin swims.
Here come a frog and a kangaroo:
I wish I could jump as high as you.
All of us happy; all of us free;
Let us all thank God for our liberty.

PRAYER

Lord of all true freedom,
Help us to be truly free.
Teach us to enjoy freely all the gifts
That you have given us.
Thank You for:
Places to go;
Things to see;
Things to hear;
Things to learn;
Things to do;
Parents, families and friends who love us;
Teachers who guide us;
Priests and pastors
Who tell us about You and Your great love for us.
Amen.

NOAH AND HIS FAMILY LEAVE THE ARK

The Ark had been a wonderful, safe home for Noah, his family and all the animals while the Great Flood lasted. Now it was time to leave the Ark which had protected them so well for so many months. In one way they felt a little sad, because it was like having to leave a faithful old friend behind. In another way they felt very happy because they had the whole wide world to live in once again. They thanked God for bringing them safely through the Great Flood and then set off to explore the world; they were full of excitement and ready for adventure.

POEM

Farewell, our strong and faithful wooden friend,
You've served us well, but this is journey's end.
Your voyage has finished on this mountain peak:
We through the world our fortunes now must seek.
We'll think and speak of you where e'er we roam,
And tell the story of our floating home.
'T will be recorded in God's Holy Word
How you once sheltered man and beast and bird.
Thousands of years from now folk still shall read
Of how you saved us in our time of need.

PRAYER

Dear Lord, teach us to be grateful.
We have so much to thank You for.
Remind us of how much we owe to You and to
  all those who help us.
Teach us to thank them properly too.
Amen.

THE RAINBOW SIGN

How beautiful God's rainbow sign
Set in the skies above:
A symbol of His beauty and
His everlasting love.

From red to orange then to gold
And green, the colours go;
Then blue and violet are seen
Each side of indigo.

PRAYER

Help us, God of all Beauty,
To see Your Beauty
In all You have made.
Put the rich colours of Your Love
Into our ordinary, everyday lives.
Make our days good and beautiful
Like Your rainbow.
We ask it for the sake
Of Jesus, our Lord.
Amen.